YOU TOO CAN CRACK UPSC CSE

A Complete Guide to Kickstart Your UPSC CSE Preparation

Naveen Kumar Chandra, IAS

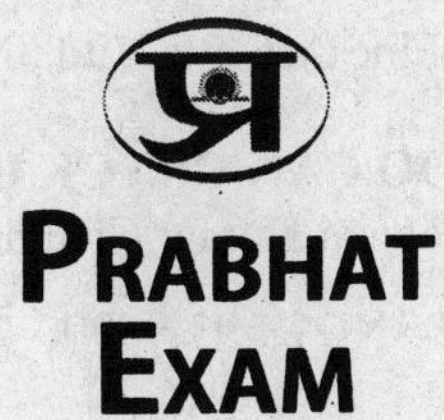

PRABHAT EXAM

Publisher
PRABHAT EXAM
Imprint of Prabhat Prakashan Pvt. Ltd.
4/19 Asaf Ali Road, New Delhi–110 002
Ph. 23289555 • 23289666 • 23289777 • Helpline/ 7827007777
e-mail: prabhatbooks@gmail.com • Website: www.prabhatexam.com

Price
Two Hundred Fifty Rupees only

ISBN 978-93-90906-79-6

Printed at
Sita Fine Arts Pvt. Ltd., New Delhi

YOU TOO CAN CRACK UPSC CSE
by Naveen Kumar Chandra, IAS

ISBN 978-93-90906-79-6

₹ 250.00

"This book, aims at doing 2 things: first, to provide the aspirants of UPSC CSE with a one stop solution to their most basic doubts, and second, to give them a solid foundation as they begin preparation. The idea of this book was mine but the execution was not mine alone. It required a lot of support and at times push from many people to finish the work. But, if I were to dedicate this book, it would surely be to, two sets of people, my family and the millions of aspirants. My family has always supported me and stood by me. They have always pushed me to do whatever I wished to and do it well. They also provided guidance whenever I needed it. This book is dedicated to all the aspirants as well, who take this leap of faith every year. I wish and hope that all those who deserve, find the success they are looking for. Thank you."

—*Naveen Kumar Chandra*

Author's Note

Having just passed out from IIT Roorkee, I had just figured out that I wanted to join the Indian Administrative Service. It had not come easy though, I had done a lot of research, which included but was not limited too, speaking to many seniors from college who were now civil servants, reading books written by civil servants, doing a lot of research on the scope and conditions of the services on internet etc. I had always believed in myself, in the sense that I would always first try to do things on my own, before asking for help, I researched about the exam on my own as well, before approaching anyone, which included books, resources, syllabus, pattern, strategy etc. But I remember that it was indeed a bit exhausting, the internet has helped for sure but too much information is a curse as well. I for one, know this first hand and know many aspirants who give months in just doing this very basic research. Hopefully, with this book, it would come to an end. All the Best!

Contents

Author's Note 5

1. How to Make a Perfect Timetable for UPSC CSE? 9

2. Notes Making for UPSC CSE: It's Importance and Lessons on Notes Making....................................50

3. Good Notes, Bad Notes......................60

4. How to Prepare Current Affairs, Newspaper Reading and Notes Making......................................79

5. Let's Make Notes and Revise Notes....99

6. GS Mains Answer Writing Essentials; The Structure 107

7. Content for a Good Answer, Books and Presentation 119

8. Value Addition 131

9. Random Thoughts 137

10. Some Fun while Preparing 144

How to Make a Perfect Timetable for UPSC CSE?

> *"Time isn't the main thing, it's the only thing."* – Miles Davis

There are a certain fixed number of hours in a day for everyone, for the successful and for those who aren't. What is it then that separates these two categories of people? Going into what makes one successful is a topic much beyond the scope of this book. For the purpose of this book, let us very narrowly define it as those who manage to clear this exam.

Well, there could be a variety of reasons, but the single most crucial factor is how they utilised their time when they still had it.

A lot of aspirants write to me regularly saying that they struggle to manage their time, that they can't seem to understand why their preparation has no direction, that they are not able to revise the syllabus properly as there is so much to study.

It is indeed the first thing which any aspirants should work on after they have read and understood the syllabus and the pattern of the exam, that is, making themselves a good timetable.

If one is to read any topper's interview or listen to any topper talk, the importance that almost all of them put on the value of time and having a good timetable is not lost on anyone. One must ask why it is so important that almost all successful candidates so insist on everyone having a timetable?

To list a few, some reasons are:

1. A good timetable, if followed religiously, will keep your preparation on track and will ensure you meet your targets.
2. It will take care of all the necessary things needed for you to do during your preparation, like revision, mocks, answer writing practice, essay writing practice etc.
3. It will give you time to unwind and relax.
4. It will ensure that you don't take too much pressure on yourself.
5. It will leave you enough time for revision and mocks only in the end.
6. It will ensure that you take care of your physical and mental health as well as create an enabling environment for you.

A good timetable is, thus, an indispensable tool. It is, though a simple looking one, but trust me, if utilized properly, it is no less than a weapon, one which will help you win this battle.

So, what are the essential components of a good timetable. If you look at the syllabus, there are many things to be covered. General Studies subjects, Optional subject, Current Affairs, CSAT etc. What then, should be the components of a timetable. Kindly have a look at the chart given below.

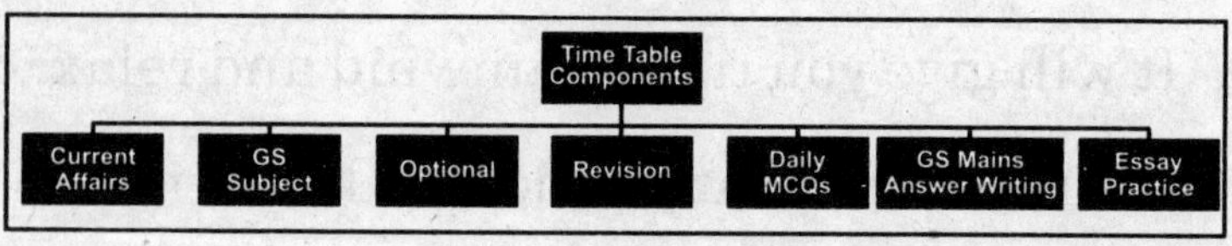

The components mentioned above are what I refer to as the 'essentials', as they are absolutely essential to your preparation. They are to be covered on a daily basis except essay practice, which is to be done weekly. You have to read current affairs from a newspaper, read a topic of any GS subject, read some of your optional subject, revise anything from the syllabus which you've already covered previously, practice

5-10 daily MCQs, write at least 1 GS-mains answer and write one essay (weekly).

All of this is to be made into a properly structured timetable. I will show the same later in the chapter. These things, if done daily, consistently and without fail for a period of 6 months, will ensure not only that you finish your syllabus in time, but will also help you revise almost 2/3rd of your syllabus, solve more than 1000 MCQs, more than 200 GS mains questions and 30 essays. This is when you don't increase their number, which you most definitely will. This is also before you formally start focusing more on mocks.

Thus, a good timetable, with all the above-mentioned components will ensure that you are ready for mains as well when you finish your preparation. If not mains, then at least for a test series and you won't be struggling initially as you start solving mock mains papers.

You might ask, how it is possible to write answers from day one when you don't know anything and haven't read enough. It is possible, and it can definitely be done, if not from day one then at least after the first few weeks. There are a number of books, which have mock and previous year mains questions divided topic-wise. You will only need to write 1-2 questions from the topic you finished that day, which would, anyway, mean you have some knowledge even if not complete information but at least something about the things asked. Then, there are many online resources which provide daily mains questions on current affairs, which again, you are reading daily. At the very beginning, content is not something you should sweat about. It won't matter much at the start, write whatever little you know. As we would discover later in the book, a good answer is not only about good content but also how you present your content. This time at the absolute start, can be used to build some skills which will fetch you extra marks.

Now, we have discussed why a good timetable is important and what the essential components of a good timetable are, let us now move forward and see how we can make one for us.

When you make a timetable, the popular way would have you work on more of a manifesto of promises that we make to ourselves, like 'Finish Economics in Next One month' or 'Write Essays Regularly' etc., these are better than having nothing but are not enough; one needs to be specific in what he/she wants to achieve, but then, one might wonder, how can we be specific about saying what is to be done in a month, one might also question that if not big goals like a subject are set in a month, how else would one keep track of the syllabus which is mostly divided into macros.

It is thus important to keep a balance, to have specific, small topics as micro targets and big subjects as a big (macro) target; it is thus advisable to adopt a strategy to have a three-layered approach when one makes his/her timetable.

This way, one can make a timetable which will be easy to follow and at the same time it will push us all to do that extra bit daily, not missing a single day, if planned in advance or not in an emergency. I call this a 3 way timetable approach. This is how it looks like:

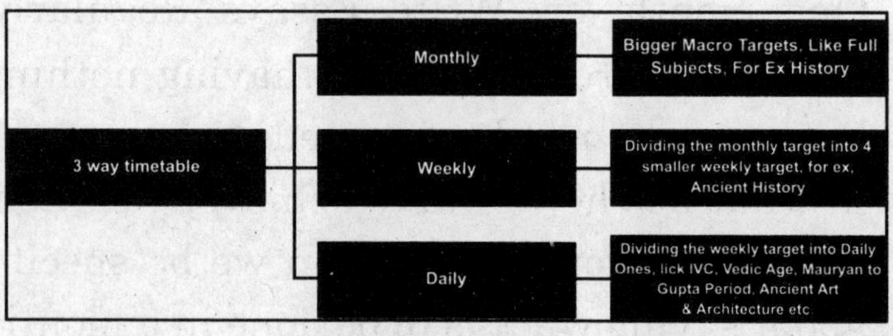

While you must have noticed by now that a good timetable, complete with a monthly, weekly and daily break-up is quite exhaustive when it comes to your syllabus but it misses one very crucial aspect and it is not just about UPSC CSE but any exam. Once you decide to prepare, advice like 'cut off from everyone', 'focus only on your goal' etc., very well might be well intentioned, but don't take these literally. Focus is absolutely important but that does not mean you don't have anything else going on in your life. Man is a social animal, we crave connecting with fellow human beings and anything otherwise is against the evolution of our species, we must thus, very carefully incorporate this aspect of our nature in our timetables.

There are various ways to do it, and it is not just about our need to meet people or interact with them which drives the necessity of us having them in our life but also the fact that we have them till now; being surrounded by people and suddenly cutting off would surely have some withdrawal symptoms, which in turn will end up affecting not just your preparation but also your mental health.

Thus, it is very important to have some time in your daily schedule for your loved ones, they may be your friends, your family or anyone you are involved with but this must be a part of your schedule. It goes without saying that you must not end up having hours long conversations but happy breaks, in a sense of a refuge. You must also understand that when I say you give your family the time they deserve, it comes back and though you might have an unconditionally loving family, but caring for them would surely make them care for you, trust me, you could not get enough of mental support during your preparation. Also, at times, and these times come for everyone, every single one, you'd find yourself down, your confidence shaken, preparation gone awry and if at this time you don't have anyone to go to, or share your insecurities or concerns with, it would soon become a very tough uphill battle.

I would strongly recommend all the aspirants, more so those who are preparing at home, to have all their meals with family and those who are staying away, to try and call friends and family after meals or any other preferred time. This very simple exercise would ensure that you stay in touch with people who care for you and whom you care for. It would also mean that the times, which believe you me, are inevitable, when you'd be down and almost out, you'll have people to help you with it. Many times, what it takes is a small nudge to keep you from getting off track, this time would help you, almost like a good investment, it would be your insurance.

Another very important aspect of this timetable is what I refer to as the 'me-time'. This is when you introspect, you ask questions to yourself, you reflect back on what's going on, from your preparation to the larger questions about how you've been feeling.

It is extremely important for you to give yourself this time, it is here that you really get time to be with yourself and seek within yourself the answers to many questions you wish and hope could be answered by others. One example would be, "Why Do I Want To Become A Civil Servant?" True, you must have had this thing clear when you started out but trust me, you'll have this doubt again and many times, if not exactly this, then some other version of it, like, "Is It Really Worth It?" or "Why Don't I Feel As Motivated As I Used To When I First Started?"

Whatever it maybe, you are going to have self-doubts, what you'd need would be some time to reflect back and find answers to these question, otherwise it would keep growing from a small self-doubt to non-belief in your abilities. This time of introspection could very well be your hobby time or a light book read or some music you like to listen or anything which makes you feel yourself, free from any target or deadline or compulsion. Ideally your preparation itself should make you feel the same, but if it doesn't, you may need this time even more.

So, we must now step back and see what are the things which must be a part of our daily schedule apart from the syllabus.

So apart from the topics that you would distribute in your timetable you must have the following as well; some time for your family or friends, some time for your hobby and some time to exercise. Yes, physical exercise is again that one thing which is indispensable, you might not get more marks but a healthier you would fall sick less often and lose lesser days, also, when you feel good about your body and your physical well-being, it transcends to your mind as well. You tend to feel good about yourself overall.

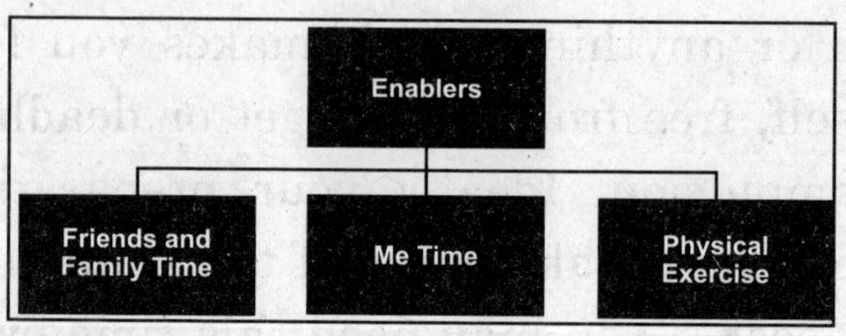

These three things are what I call 'enablers'; they enable you to give your best every time.

Once you have all the components needed for your timetable, you must decide the outline, the overall look, a few important pointers for the same would be:

1. Try not to have a session last more than an hour because our concentration starts coming down after 45-50 minutes and we can no longer grasp much of what we read.

2. Always try to have small breaks in between your sessions, it could be a song or a walk or anything but take a small

break after every 45-50 minutes of around 10 minutes.

3. Always eat your meals on time and have good, wholesome meals and not junk food. This is again to ensure that you don't make clearing UPSC CSE an end in itself, when there indeed are much more important things in life. Your health is one of them.
4. Always get a minimum of 7-8 hours of sleep every day and ensure you get a sound sleep, you may try to read a light book before bed.
5. As you go to sleep, avoid any screen time (laptop, mobile etc.) for at least an hour before you go to bed.

We have till now, discussed what all you have to keep in mind to make a timetable, these are:

But you might ask, well, how can a college student and a working professional follow the same rules when it comes to their timetable, it's a good point.

But I am trying to help everyone with the macros of a good timetable, one would need to use them and modify them as per their own requirement. That's why I don't talk as much about the number of hours as all of us have a different number of them free but I do talk about how to use the free hours you have.

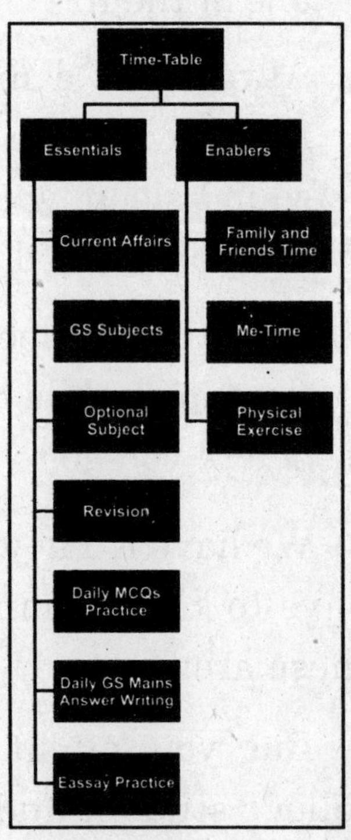

I would now try to help three main categories of people who prepare for UPSC CSE with a timetable, viz. full-time aspirants, college students and working professionals. I would obviously make some assumptions, none so dramatic that you won't be able to use the timetable. Yet, the timetable has been deciphered in much detail above, you may use all that information to make one for yourself from scratch.

The most common category is that of full-time aspirants, students who are preparing for the UPSC CSE examination and have opted not to work anywhere and have finished college. I too belonged to the same category, I had started preparing after I finished college and had opted not to take up a job, I didn't sit for campus placements and started my preparation in a week or so after I got back home. Though this category of aspirants has the maximum amount of time in their hands, this is also a curse at times.

The amount of time which appears too much is not actually too much, with more time, one has more things to manage and one also has the added pressure of preparing full-time and much higher expectations of succeeding. Thus, it is very important to have a time table which is very efficient and also very effective, that is not only one has to ensure that he/she gives good time to his/her preparation but also that the time he/she gives is utilized in the best way as possible.

Before going into some details for a timetable of a full time aspirant, I would make some assumptions, like the aspirant is preparing full-time without any job of any kind, that he or she is preparing by self-study this because a vast majority of the aspirants in fact prepare on their own, (it looks counter intuitive but it's true as most just can't afford the expensive fees of coaching institutes). For all others who are preparing with coaching, it is very easy to modify the time table I'd suggest for the self-studying aspirants. I'll tell how to do it as well. I would make one month timetable for a full-time aspirant and assume he/ she has Political Science and International

Relations as optional subject. One can easily replace it with their own optional subject. I would also assume that one has at least 7-8 months in hands, as in 7-8 months for prelims exam. I would also assume that one is a fresher at UPSC CSE, that is, it is their first attempt, but again, it can easily be modified to suit anyone with any amount of experience.

So, for example, in the first month of the preparation, we would be studying GS History, PSIR optional paper 1, current affairs and solving MCQs, practicing some answer writing (to begin in last week) and writing a couple of essays. Also, a typical day would include 7 hours of sleep, 1 hour of physical exercise, 1 hour for hobbies, 3 hours for other activities, this would leave 12 hours. We would aim at studying topics for 8 hours and 1.5 hours would be kept for revision (to begin from second day) and 30 minutes for MCQs and 1 hour for answer writing.

Thus, this is how a good overall timetable (Based on the 3 way timetable approach) should look like:

Monthly Time Table: Month 1

- History NCERT books, Reference Books with notes making.
- PSIR paper 1 part A complete with making notes.
- Revision of at least 3/4th of the topics covered in the month.
- Current affairs from newspaper, one website and one magazine for whole month.
- Around 200-250 MCQs on current affairs and GS topics covered.
- 3-4 essays.
- 20 GS mains questions.

Weekly Timetable: Week 1

- Ancient History- Stone Age, IVC, Vedic, Post Vedic, Haryanka, Shishunaga,

Nandas, Mauryas, Shunga, Kanva, Guptas, Foreign Invasions and Dynasties of foreign origin, Sangam Period and South Indian Dynasties, Buddhism, Jainism, Cults & Sects, ancient schools of philosophy.

- PSIR- political theory, theories of state
- Revision of GS and Optional.
- Current affairs of the topics studied in the week.
- 50-70 MCQs of the topics studied.
- 1 essay.

Daily Timetable: Day 1

Before I write this, I am again assuming that you have done all basic research about the exam, are familiar with the syllabus and topics and pattern.

Things to be done:

- Ancient History- Stone Age, IVC, Vedic period.

- PSIR- Political theory (3 sub topics).
- Revise the same thing covered the same day (only for day 1).
- Newspaper, Current Affairs from a website.
- 10 MCQs on Current affairs, MCQs on the topics covered from a book which has topic wise MCQs.
- Gym or running or any other physical exercise.
- Hobby or me-time.
- Sleep.

Detailed Daily Schedule

Wake up	5:00 AM
Reach Gym and Workout	Till 6:30 AM
Get Back and have Breakfast	Till 7:20 AM
Current Affairs	7:30 AM- 9:00 AM
Break	Till 09:15 AM

Ancient History	9:15 AM- 10:15 AM
Break	Till 10:30 AM
Ancient History	10:30 AM- 11:30 AM
Break	Till 11:45 AM
Ancient History	11:45 AM- 12:45 AM
Lunch Break	Till 1:30 PM
PSIR Optional	1:30 PM- 2:30 PM
Break	Till 2:45 PM
PSIR Optional	2:45 PM- 3:45 PM
Break	Till 4:00 PM
PSIR Optional	4:00 PM- 5:00 PM
'Me-Time' Break	Till 6 PM
MCQs Practice	6:00 PM- 6:30 PM
Revision	6:30 PM- 7:30 PM
Break	Till 7:45 PM

GS Mains Answer writing	7:45 PM- 8:15 PM
Making Next Days' Timetable	Till 8:30 PM
Dinner and Family Time	Till 9:30 PM
Go to Bed	By 10:00 PM

So, as one can see, this timetable is pretty exhaustive, it covers GS, Optional subject, current affairs, MCQs, Revision and also has scope to add or subtract things. At the same time, the timetable also takes care of your exercise, meals, proper sleep and hobby time.

Thus, it provides you a fine balance between studies and everything else. It would ensure that you have time for everything you need to have a fit body and a fit mind.

It is advised that small breaks are taken but at times we get in what is known as the state of 'flow', wherein we are very focused and would rather continue what we are doing as the productivity is very high, in such a scenario, one can go ahead and stretch one patch to 2-3 hours and then take a 15-20 minutes break.

One might also feel that they don't need an hour-long break for lunch and dinner and maybe 30-45 minutes are good enough, again, you may shorten that and create one more period of 45-60 minutes and use it for optional or GS, whichever you feel needs more time.

Then again, one might also want to note that gym or any other exercise is to be done 5 or 6 days a week, as the body needs time to recover, and on the off, days the time can be utilized again as per one's convenience and need.

I would also like to advise all the students who are staying say in a PG or hostel and have to cook food and manage other things on their own; it is advisable to prepare meals at one go, at least breakfast and lunch, similarly, keep Sundays for things like laundry etc. and time saved from gym can be used here.

This is to give one an idea on how to go about making a timetable, almost no one's would look like this, mine didn't either but it was very close and same should be your strategy, to get as much organized as possible. Once you are organized and have control over the things, things would start looking much easier and possible. Your confidence would also remain high when you would see yourself meeting small daily targets and moving towards the bigger weekly and monthly ones. You must understand and realize that these timetables are all interlinked and as you keep meeting daily targets you would never miss weekly and as you meet weekly targets you would never miss the monthly ones, Thus, in a matter of 6 intensive months, you'd be able to finish the syllabus very thoroughly and then you'd have enough time to focus only on revision, mocks and answer writing practice.

For Working Professionals

Time table for working professionals is a task; the biggest issue is the lack of time and the dual responsibility. It can't be assumed that once they get off from work, all the time they have can be given to preparation but that's a sacrifice they have to make. They have to find every single minute they can manage and use it well. They too must find time for their own self, their health and this makes the task even tougher. That is why, for working professional, weekends are much more important. The use of commute time and breaks in office become very valuable and parties and outings become a luxury. It is obvious that this has to be done only for a limited period and once they finish the syllabus they can get back to a more relaxed timetable. It must also be accepted that no matter what, they can't finish the syllabus in the same amount of time as a full time aspirant and they would need to rely on things like video lectures as they can be useful while commuting. They may also like to use this one strategy which a few people use for effective revision, they may like to record their voice when they read a topic for the first time and listen to it when they travel and thus use the same for effective revision.

Now, if we assume an 8-hour work day and another 2 hours for commuting, 1 hour for breakfast and dinner, 7 hours sleep, 1 hour for exercise, we are left with only 5 hours, out of which one can be expected to study for a maximum of 4 hours. So, while a full-time aspirant gets anywhere between 10-12 hours free, a working professional has 4 hours in hand. That is why the commute time and the breaks in office are to be used effectively. But much more than this, the time one gets on weekends is to be used, one has to try and compensate for the less time on weekdays. They would thus need to give 14 hours on weekends and with 4 hours on each of the weekdays, they would have around 48 hours in total and add to that the commute time and breaks in office, it could be as high as 65+ hours, which is very close to the 75+ odd hours a full-time aspirant gets.

Now, this is all for illustrative purposes and real number of hours for a working professional could be way lower as they might not get any break or any way to study while commuting, in such a condition, they would need to prepare for a longer time, need to be very precise with their preparation and take some intelligent risks. Like they could do without the newspaper and solely rely on a monthly magazine, they need not study all the NCERTs and start directly with reference books, they may like to opt for an optional subject which has a wider overlap with GS subjects and syllabus and they would like to join test series earlier and not leave mocks and practice for later part of the preparation. For working professional, more than full time aspirants, it is important to have very limited resources, to be covered thoroughly. I can't lay anymore stress on the effective use of time, there is no need at all to read same thing from multiple sources, no matter who says it, there is no need to make notes of newspaper if you are also reading a monthly magazine, there is no need to just pile on study material, most of it is repetitive, no need to read multiple types of current affairs compilations etc.

So, for a working professional, on weekends, their timetable would look like that of a full time aspirant, with the following changes:

Wake up	5:00 AM
Reach Gym and Workout	Till 6:30 AM
Get Back and have Breakfast	Till 7:20 AM
Current Affairs	7:30 AM- 9:00 AM
Break	Till 09:15 AM
Ancient History	9:15 AM- 10:15 AM
Break	Till 10:30 AM
Ancient History	10:30 AM- 11:30 AM
Break	Till 11:45 AM
Ancient History	11:45 AM- 12:45 AM
Lunch Break	Till 1:30 PM
PSIR Optional	1:30 PM- 2:30 PM
Break	Till 2:45 PM
PSIR Optional	2:45 PM- 3:45 PM
Break	Till 4:00 PM

PSIR Optional	4:00 PM- 7:00 PM
'Me-Time' Break	Till 7:30 PM
MCQs Practice	7:30 PM- 8:00 PM
Revision	8:00 PM- 9:00 PM
Break	Till 9:15 PM
GS Mains Answer writing	9:15 PM- 9:45 PM
Making Next Days' Timetable	Till 10:00 PM
Dinner and Family Time	Till 10:45 PM
Go to Bed	By 11:00 PM

In the timetable above, a working professional is supposed to sleep 6 hours and some time has been taken off from dinner and 'me-time'. These small sacrifices are to be made and one really has no choice.

While it might seem harsh and at one level it is. What one also needs to understand is that a full-time aspirant has different kinds of sacrifices to make. Many are well qualified and well placed to take up a job but they decide to sacrifice it and with it the financial stability it offers, not just to them but their family.

For a weekday, assuming office hours from 9 AM-5 PM and commute time from 8 AM to 9 AM in the morning and 5 PM to 6 PM in the evening, would look like this:

Wake up	4:30 AM
Reach Gym and Workout	Till 6:00 AM
Get Back and have Breakfast	Till 6:45 AM
GS History	6:45 AM- 7:45 AM
Commute to office (GS History Video lectures on the way)	8:00 AM- 9:00 AM
Office Hours (Try to find 30 min to 1 hour in office, in small breaks, for GS Current Affairs)	9:00 AM- 5:00 PM

Commute Back Home (Video Lectures on Optional Subject)	Till 6 PM
Freshen Up	By 6:30 PM
GS History	6:30 PM- 7:30 PM
Break	Till 7:45 PM
GS Mains Answer writing and MCQs (half hour each)	7:45 PM- 8:45 PM
Making Next Days' Timetable	Till 9:00 PM
Dinner and Family Time	Till 9:30 PM
Go to Bed	By 10:00 PM

Again, all of this is to show how you can make a timetable for yourself. Many things might differ and they can easily be substituted. If at all it is too tough, my advice would be to give 1 year to UPSC, not more than that and see if you can manage without a job. Only one year as after that, even if you are not able to clear the exam, you wouldn't need to study full time to prepare and also one year gap would not affect your job chances.

For a College Students

Aspirants wanting to start off early are not a new thing but ever since more and more candidates started getting selected right after college, in their first attempts, many students want to start their preparation in college itself.

They hope to spread their preparation over the years of their graduation and take their graduation side by side. This they feel, gives them an edge over those who start after their college, but it makes little if any sense, I'll try to explain.

Common sense would tell you that no matter when someone started their preparation, they are appearing in the exam having prepared for it, whether one prepared for it after college or one does it while still in college make no difference. The only benefit one might say is that someone getting selected right after college stands a chance at getting early into the service, which again, is not that great a gain, considering one can enter just one year later if one prepares after graduating. One might say what is the chance of getting selected in one year's preparation and that too in first attempt, turns out; chances of getting selected right after college are even lower.

Still, for all those interested, I would lay down certain rules they can follow while making a timetable and a strategy for themselves when they are in college. But, while you make yourself this timetable, do keep in mind the following points:

1. That you have a wonderful opportunity in front of you, a very large number of students still don't get to go to a college and you are fortunate, don't waste this wonderful learning opportunity.

2. College studies are not to be taken lightly, some might say that what use would be say Mass Transfer and Heat Transfer in the IAS, well, to be honest you never know but even if not of direct use, doing well at it makes you a better student, gets you into the habit of taking things in your plate seriously.

3. UPSC has graduation as the minimum qualification; this is of course enough for you to understand that graduation is thus valued by UPSC. They see it as a value adding experience to your personality, some qualities they deem and think important for a civil servant to have.

4. College time is the peak of your youth, when you are not afraid of taking risks and learning new things, use this time to explore many subjects, hobbies, interests etc. and try to gain as much knowledge as possible. Learning from one's own experience is the best learning there is.

5. In no way are you going to get this time again, you won't get any time again unless you build a time machine but this time is extra valuable, live it and don't just make it about an exam.
6. Working on your personality, trying to widen your horizon and gaining perspective, college time is the best time to do all this.

Now, having said all of the above, I would strongly recommend that don't start your preparation in 1st or 2nd year of your college (assuming a 4 years course). Reasons are many but most importantly, you'll be attempting the exam after 3 years, if you begin preparing in the 1st or 2nd year, quite simply, the pattern might have changed by the time you would actually write the exam, the syllabus might have also changed, optional subjects might no longer be there (since their exclusion has been a matter of huge debate for quite some time now). Basically, you never know what will happen 3 years from now, in such a case, it would be almost cruel to spread the preparation of 6-7 months over 3-4 years. Moreover, you'd get bored and maybe even impatient and disillusioned with the exam.

Then, one of the most beautiful part of UPSC CSE is that you get to read so many new things and you are excited, this excitement is very hard to be maintained for 3-4 years. It is thus desirable that you start in the 3rd year of your college and start with basics (NCERTs and newspaper) and try to finish them (NCERTs) in the 1st semester and then gradually move on to the reference books of GS and Optional paper and finish them in the next 2 semesters, while the last one is kept reserved only for revision and mocks.

For college students, it must be kept in mind that they need not compromise on either their studies or their fun. UPSC CSE must not make you drift away from friends or get you isolated, it must also not become the reason for poor marks in college or missing out on fun activities or sports that you would've otherwise participated in.

Trust me, it harms much more than it ever stands a chance to benefit. The reason is that you miss out on something which is right there for something which is far and has no guarantee that you'll have it, it is harsh but true. An exam with lakhs of aspirants and a handful of vacancies, is bound to end on a sad note for many, it is up to us that it does not also end leaving us disillusioned and in the middle of nowhere. Also, ignoring college is not good even if you manage to get selected. I am sure that the nation doesn't need officers who would, while working on an assignment, are thinking of a possible future assignment which they find more desirable and thus, are not giving their 100% to the job in hand.

In short, use the first and second year of your college to develop a reading habit, read as much possible and as wide a variety of books as possible. Try to gain as many perspectives as possible, this would be an asset even in the preparation, when you finally start full time. It is true that the exam is subjective, but what is also true is that the exam is fair, there are things which makes your chances better and trust me, doing good at college would make you a better student and this in turn would help in your preparation.

Not to say that those who perform average in college or school won't get selected but they would surely need to develop the habit of studying and working hard and would need extra effort.

Notes Making for UPSC CSE: It's Importance and Lessons on Notes Making

Notes making for UPSC CSE, is one of the most common trouble areas for aspirants. Many aspirants struggle with different aspects of making notes. While most agree it is indeed important to make notes, many still end up looking for shortcuts, it may be looking for the topper's notes or not making notes at all and relying on books completely.

Well, whatever be the reason or refuge, they are not justified. As we shall see, our own notes are very important as it is not just the notes but the process of making them that is a learning experience and almost no selected candidate would ask you to not make your own notes yourself.

One of the most fundamental reasons why making notes is essential is the fact that the syllabus is huge and we are required to read so many books and study materials. One cannot expect to be reading entire books again and again when they sit for revision, they won't ever have that much time, it would be a huge waste of time and resources.

While reading books again might look a decent solution, it never is. Books are to be read to clear your concepts and to revisit if you get stuck somewhere. Notes on the other hand, are precise and you write only the most relevant and important things from the books in your notes, for quick and multiple revisions.

Books are too bulky at times and you can't carry them wherever you wish, notes are precise and concise, they can be carried anywhere one wishes to carry them. Then, with notes, things may be added later or removed, they offer a scope to work with them as your preparation goes on. Books on the other hand must only be kept for reading once and as reference.

While some books indeed are written so precisely that it's impossible to make even more precise notes out of them, some are very well written but do contain many things which are not important from the point of view of UPSC CSE and may be needed to be avoided.

It must be kept in mind that this exam is meant to be taken as an exam and not a thesis topic, one need not become an UPSC syllabus books collector and have all the books on every topic recommended by every topper and also keep in mind that one is dealing with text books and not fiction, it is desirable to make short notes.

Another very important aspect and for me the most important one with respect to notes making, more so in the context of UPSC CSE preparation is that they help you in developing an answer writing habit. Getting you acquainted with the various dimensions of writing, notes polish your writing skills and get you in the habit of using various components and tools to explain or write about a topic. When you draw diagrams or make flow charts in your notes, they come more naturally to you in your answers, when you try to explain a concept in least number of words, it makes you practice for word limit.

Similarly, making notes also helps you improve in your general writing skills, be it grammar, spellings and other very basic things needed to write good answers. You get into the habit of writing and thus when you do finally write GS mocks for written exam, you don't get exhausted by the time you are half way. Answer writing, like we will discuss in detail in the book later, is in itself a great exercise and making notes makes it easier.

Writing skills are not something which comes naturally to all of us, while some enjoy writing and get a hold of it easily, others struggle with writing even a few lines on the easiest of topics by themselves when they can go on and on about it while speaking.

It is thus advised to write as much as possible and as often as possible, more so while preparing for CSE. Making Notes is probably the best way to do it. I can imagine one at least getting familiar with sentence formations, getting better at grammar and familiar with writing in both paragraphs and points, at the same time using things like diagrams.

Another important aspect of making notes comes from the fact that revision is as important as reading new topics for this exam. The syllabus is so big that without regular revision it is impossible to retain so much information. One must do it regularly and notes are the perfect tools to do it efficiently and effectively. Revision is something you can do while traveling and carrying notes with yourself in your bag is always much easier than say a book.

It is also very good to glance through major topics, mostly covered in a few pages in your notes which would otherwise take turning many pages in a book and thus a lot more time and effort. Always carrying some notes wherever you go is a great way to utilize all the commute time, good, precise notes are always helpful.

It is almost unimaginable to revise effectively without having made your own notes. It must also be noted that the exercise of making own notes itself makes you revise many things as you read the topic multiple times when you make notes out of it. You also tend to understand it better as you try to write on the relevant portion and get maximum value out of your own notes. Thus, you start benefitting right from the very beginning by the exercise of notes making and you always get something good out of it.

To explain the importance of your own notes and notes in general, let us take a look at an illustration. Imagine you have cleared CSE prelims in your first attempt and you are at the centre of your written exam. You know that over the next 7 days, you'll be writing a lot of papers that cover a huge amount of syllabus and a wide variety of topics. You don't want to miss out and have this urge of revising one last time (trust me, last minute revisions are, at times, important confidence boosters).

But, how would you ever revise the whole paper's worth of syllabus in just the break between 2 GS papers, which is only a couple of hours. Well, if you have your own notes, which are much concise than the whole books, you'd at least stand a chance of glancing over a huge portion of the syllabus and have things fresh in your memory.

I am not saying that revising at this point is important or even required but most aspirants do revise some or the other topics and it is always better to have short and crisp notes to do the same. It is also important to note that for revision in the last one month of either the prelims or the mains it is absolutely crucial that you have notes as you would like to revise the syllabus multiple times and it would also be important to revise the whole syllabus and not just some portions.

It is not a mere coincidence that almost all the toppers lay equal amount of stress on the importance of notes making. In fact, it is very rare, almost non-existent for a topper to ever say that he/she never made any notes at all or relied completely on notes of other selected candidates or coaching institutes or that they read directly from the book every time they had to revise or revisit a concept.

It is not by mere chance that people are always looking for 'topper's notes' when in fact they must realize that they are toppers because they made notes themselves and thus, they themselves need to do the same if they want to get selected like the people they look up to.

Relying on someone else's notes is never advisable anyway, only as an exception it may be, for topics too small and too specific. As notes making is a very personal exercise, in the sense that notes are to be, most importantly, accessible to that one person who makes them and not everyone else. I, for example, make notes in a way that suits me the best. The basic outline might very well remain the same for everyone or most, but what goes inside and in the details, might vary as I might need only a keyword to be written for a topic while someone else might want the entire definition. Though it is not advisable to write all definitions but then everyone has their own pace of learning, this much subjectivity is natural.

Another reason why it is not fine to completely rely on someone else's notes is that when anyone makes their own notes, they apply their mind in such a way that it would help them to remember the tougher topics better. So that, when they revise from their notes these tougher topics, they are able to recollect them better, making it easier for them to revise them with more attention to them and more focus on them.

Thus, making notes is not only important and desirable but it is indispensable if one wants to take no chances with one's preparation and wants to be as sure as possible.

Good Notes, Bad Notes

Having discussed the importance of notes making from various standpoints, it is now time to look into the subject a bit more deeply. What is it that makes a set of notes good, when I say good, I don't mean beautiful to look at, it's not a beauty pageant for notes, but what I mean is useful.

What makes them good is that they are good enough for your preparation. Making notes is not easy, I mean it's fairly intuitive to know what one means by notes, it means to extract the important points from any topic, add your own insight if any and write them down for future reference. But, it is not that easy to execute or actually make them. There are many reasons for it, most aspirants take the notes making exercise as an end in itself, that is, they feel that notes making exercise itself will get them selected or is that crucial when in fact it is just a tool, a very important one but in the end it is only a tool for your success.

Thus, it makes no difference at all that you use five different coloured pens or a pencil, that you use a ruler to draw lines or you don't have any, that you use sticky notes to mark pages or not, that you use a very beautiful cursive handwriting or one which would make a medico blush, none of this actually matters.

At the very beginning when we are to discuss what makes a set of notes useful, I would first like to list some points which don't matter when you make notes or that they won't make your notes more or less useful:

1. No need to worry about handwriting till it's legible. Your handwriting in the actual written exam matters to the extent that it is legible and that examiner would not be required to put in extra efforts to only understand what you have written. Thus, it is advisable to make notes in the same handwriting that you would be comfortable in having in your actual mains examination, prepare yourself for that. It must also be kept in mind that time shortage almost always would make you write in a handwriting which would be worse than what you had planned but that must be factored in.

2. No one cares for 4-5 different colours of pens. Unless you have 4-5 times than the time an average aspirant does, this exercise is better avoided and even if you do have it, there are no extra marks for it.

3. There is no such thing is 'very important', 'important' and 'less important', what I mean is, don't make superficial categories in your notes, it would inadvertently make you focus more on one and less on other points. If at all you feel that a point is not that important but feel 'unsafe' in leaving it out, write it, just write it and don't categorize it. As you progress, you'd be able to judge better what is to be left out and what is to be added, don't panic.
4. It is a new area for you, you haven't been preparing for the exam for years, you might not even have studied most of the subjects, so, if you feel that you are getting stuck in making notes, it's absolutely fine. It is absolutely natural for you to get stuck unless you are a black hole and nothing can escape from you.
5. Don't start comparing your notes with those of fellow aspirants, don't get intimidated by the beautiful notes of other students, and don't feel that your notes are inferior

because they lack the colour scheme or grid patterns or are sticky notes all over the place.

6. You may like to refer toppers' notes if you wish but only to see and gain perspective on how they approached a topic and how you can make your future notes say more precise or useful content-wise. It must be seen that you only look them up for inspiration and not copying them, again, toppers' notes would be useful for you only for two reasons, you may learn from their mistakes and their best practices which you find suitable to your way of doing things, nothing else.

Now, once you keep in mind the things mentioned above, you are good to go. You are ready to make your own notes. You must though try to remember a few key points needed to make your notes more effective. Remember, making notes is also making you ready for answer writing, thus, we would focus on this aspect also when we get down to making notes.

Set of notes, mostly, would be based on the following key points:

1. Use of Key Words

If you are reading a new subject, it is quite possible that in a very short piece of writing you might find a lot of words equally important. But it is never the case, you would always have a few key words which would make your notes less cluttered and give it more weight and also their exclusion would be detrimental for your notes and answers.

I would like to explain it further with an example, say you are studying the concept of what is called as the 'invisible hand' in economics, now you might come across a broad definition with a detailed analysis and examples to make it clear for the reader that what exactly the concept means. But, you can make your notes on this concept by using a handful of words. You may write- ‘market forces- supply and demand determining and driving equilibrium’.

This small phrase has all the key words needed for you to understand the concept of the invisible hand. I must caution here that I am talking about GS Notes and the same topic for Economics optional might need a more technical definition and thus a few more keywords and detail.

What is also to be kept in mind is that keywords are a must when you write about a concept in your GS answers, as they are at the very foundation of the concept and an examiner would always look for them.

Examiners have many copies to correct and looking for keywords saves their time and tells them that you are aware of the most important things in the topic.

Then, making notes this way would make your notes much more precise and concise and would also get you into the habit of coming to the point directly and not missing out something important or relegating it to the last.

2. Be Precise

I have the luxury to be writing a book about UPSC CSE preparation and I have still chosen to write one which doesn't beat around the bush but rather comes straight to the most important points. It is hardly 200 odd pages though I had the luxury to write as much as I wished, you don't want to read more than what is absolutely important.

Precision means to be as close to the truth as possible, it means that you must be as close to what the examiner wants to see in the exam. Thus, making notes must be done in a way that it makes you ready for this. It means that if they want you to, say, define a particular subjective concept, say poverty, what you need to understand is, though there may be a lot of technical definitions or approaches to studying poverty, in essence it means state of inability in the face of willingness to afford and live a dignified life. This much in your notes is enough to define poverty.

What is dignified may vary according to approaches but all agree on its presence in the definition. It may also include various elements but that's secondary definition and not important to say or write when asked to define poverty.

Thus, a precise note would have you not beat around the bush but come straight to the most important and central point or idea.

3. Be Concise

To say a lot in a few words is an art, comes naturally to the poets but if I'd say that you'll have to become a poet to write concise notes, it would be an exaggeration.

Since we already are aware that word limit in the written exam are important and they are put in place to check if you have the ability to send across your points in a very concise way. More often than not, if you are well prepared, you would find yourself with extra material and extra points but limited time and space (not be confused with spacetime where you might view the time in your hand differently).

What would you do in such a scenario, you would need to be in practice of writing in a way where you say all that you want to or the most that you want to and use lesser words.

Let me give you an example, if you are to write a few lines on say the famous scientist Albert Einstein, you might write, "Albert Einstein was a world-famous physicist, he was born in Germany. He won the Nobel Prize in Physics for his discovery of the laws of the photoelectric effect. He is well known for his contributions to theoretical physics, especially his theories of Special Relativity and General Relativity." This is a well written note or paragraph on the personality but can we make it more concise for our notes? Yes, let's see, we may instead write, "Albert Einstein- Germany born theoretical Physicist, Discovered Special and General Relativity, Nobel Winner for Photoelectric Effect."

The two paragraphs have the exact same information, one looks like a description from an article while the other looks like someone made short notes on him. The second one, the note, is only 15 words, 1/3rd of the first one, with exact same information, which means, I can write twice as many words more and still it'll be shorter than the first paragraph.

Thus, making concise notes would help you in getting in more points, making your notes leaner and much easier to revise. Making notes is as important as you revise via your notes and you get into the habit of handling questions in the way your notes answers them. Thus, a set of notes which has whole paragraphs from a book copy pasted, would hardly make you ready to write the same concept in lesser words.

You'd waste a lot of time thinking what's important and what's not and in the process you would most definitely miss out on some important points. Making concise notes is an exercise in training your mind. When your notes say a lot in lesser words, you revise more effectively and you save a lot of time, it's a win-win for you from all aspects.

It would benefit you even after you enter the services, the habit of being concise.

4. Use Tools Like flow Charts and Tables

How do you make notes of a chapter which is 25 pages long and each page has 300 words in 2-3 pages? Not possible if you are not going to use flowcharts and/or tables to make your notes lean and save a lot of space and words.

Whatever you wish to write in your notes, in say points under a heading can easily be converted to a flowchart, which is not just easy to revise but also, saves you space and words for more points, saves you time when you revise and make your notes leaner and shorter. It also gets you into the habit of using the same or similar charts in your mains answers and thus saving a lot of time and space there as well.

It is not tough either, just remember the lessons above, keywords, precision and concise writing and you would be able to convert any otherwise points or paragraph-based note into a flow chart based one. What it also does is that it gives your notes a more structured look and also gives your thoughts a more structured look. It shows that you know how to manage your thoughts, get them together and present them in an easy to understand way.

It makes a good impression, this of course is for the answers but for the notes, it saves a lot of time when you'll be revising. Flow charts, when made properly follow a logical pattern and are effective to revise things in a logical sequence and remember the chain of events, more so in history, polity etc.

To give one example, let us see how a flow chart would look like when we write the same things in a point wise, paragraph wise and a flow chart way.

First, the paragraph:

UPSC CSE

"The exam pattern of UPSC CSE is fairly simple but very comprehensive. It is conducted in 2 stages, Preliminary and Mains, the Mains is further divided into 2 stages, the written exam and personality test. The preliminary exam has 2 papers, both of them are objective and both carry 200 marks each. One of them is General Studies and the other one is CSAT.

GS paper marks are counted in declaring the cut off, while CSAT is only qualifying in nature.

Similarly, the written part of the mains examination has both qualifying and merit papers, it has 4 GS papers, 1 essay paper which are common for all, 2 optional papers which may vary, depending upon the subject chosen by the candidate, an English language qualifying paper and a regional language qualifying paper. Only those who clear the cut off are eligible to appear for the personality test, held in an interview format.

Marks of both the written exam and the personality test are added to declare the final result and ranks in the merit list."

Now, let's see how this information may look like in a chart:

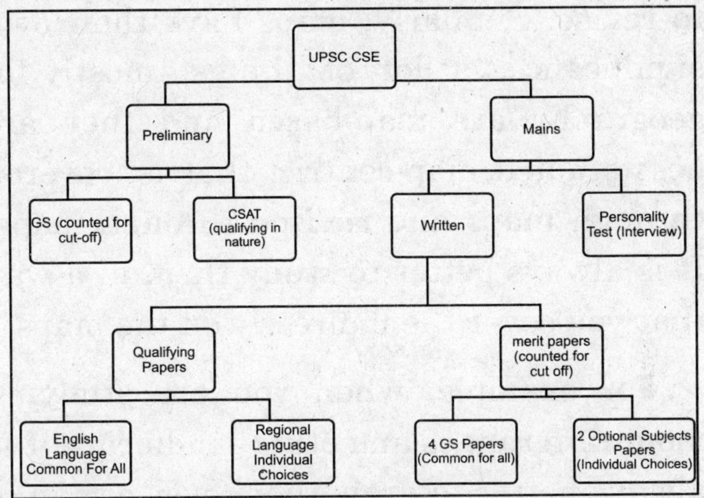

So, we have represented the same set of information in 2 ways. It is clear that the flow chart make it much easier and faster to read and comprehend the same amount of information. It is also clear that they make the presentation better, more appealing and at the same time make it look more professional.

5. Maps and Diagrams

Diagrams, much like flow charts, act as a value adding tool by enhancing the presentation. Also, they save a lot of space, give your notes an extra dimension and make them leaner and also a lot easier to revise. Similarly, maps have their own significance, a lot of things, mostly in geography are map-based and they are best studied map-centric, that is, covered through maps and revised through maps. It is always better to study them in a way that you cover them directly on the maps.

For example, when you are studying mountain ranges and other landforms, it is always better to draw them over a map of India and see there where they meet and in which states they are. It is much better to visualise geography, it remains in your memory longer, and images tend to stay longer than text.

These are yet another important addition which would add a lot of value to your notes and in turn your answers.

When you draw a diagram to support what you are trying to say, it does 2 things, first it shows the extra effort you are willing to make, second, it conveys your message more clearly, so much so that a good diagram will almost all the times mean what you've written won't matter that much and you'll be awarded good marks.

It is obvious that in some cases, it can backfire, a diagram for the sake of it might take attention away from the good content you've written. So, be careful in what you draw and if you draw. But it is no doubt true that relevant diagrams would get you extra marks.

Let us try to see an example, if I am to make notes of a geographical concept or topic with maps and diagrams, what would be the result:

This is a Map representing Indian Monsoon. Now, if I was to write about the winds and their directions with respect to Indian Monsoon, it would not have made such an impact. It is very important for you to understand, that for a topic which can be better represented with the help of a map or a diagram, it is wise to do so.

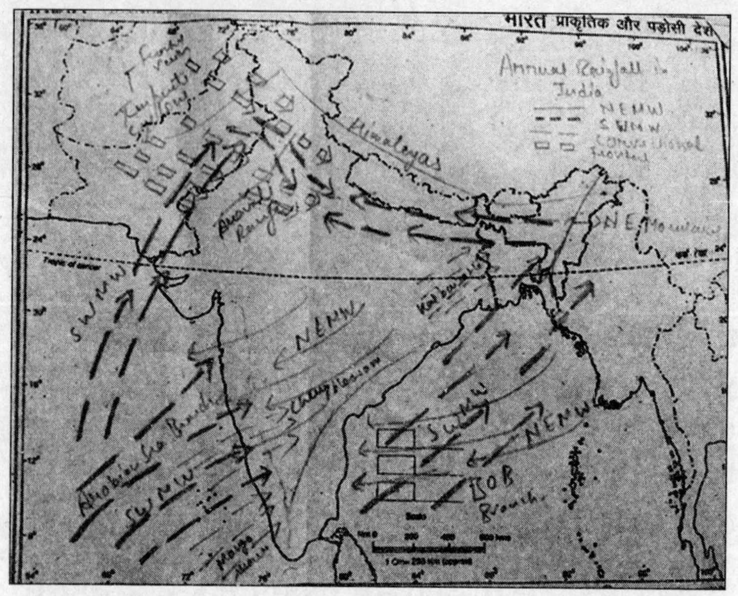
भारत प्राकृतिक और पड़ोसी देश
Annual Rainfall in India
NEMW
SWMW
Himalayas
NEMW
SWMW
SWMW
NEMW
BOB Branch
Tropic of cancer

How to Prepare Current Affairs, Newspaper Reading and Notes Making

Current affairs have come to occupy the central point for UPSC CSE preparation and they have become the most important part of the syllabus. They are important not just for prelims but for all stages of the examination and almost all the papers. You would find it useful to either use them in your answers or you might as well find a direct question based on recent events, in any paper.

Current affairs have thus come to play the most important role in the preparation with their dynamic nature and their application, a point which is not lost on any coaching institute.

If we look into it, current affairs are important for the following reasons:

1. Direct questions from recent events might be asked in prelims, mains or interview.
2. You might need to use the knowledge of current affairs in a concept to give it a contemporary dimension and make it more relatable.
3. You might need to explain a phenomenon in history with current events to show its relevance.
4. Current examples in subjects like IR, Ethics, and Polity etc. are very valuable as they show that you have the ability to link concept with its application and see how it plays out.

5. As an administrator, you are expected to know and be aware of the recent events and this makes them even more important, in the eyes of the examiner.

Current affairs for UPSC CSE are not to be mistaken for general knowledge, they are two different things. Current affairs are wider in their scope and they are mostly very conceptual in their appeal. They would not be about a plain fact, in most cases. Another way to look at it would be to say that all general knowledge is current affairs but not all current affairs are general knowledge.

I would like to give one example to make my point, take for example the following statement, "Taj Mahal was built by Shah Jahan and it is situated in Agra", this is a typical general knowledge statement, while if I were to say, "Taj Mahal is a great example of Mughal Architecture which is an amalgamation of Persian, Islamic, Turkish and Indian architecture, it was built by Shah Jahan who was a patron of art and architecture and is situated in Agra", now it's not just the slight detail about the architecture which makes it relevant, it is just an example to show that an UPSC CSE aspirant is expected to know more than just the superficial. They are supposed to be aware, not just informed.

Current affairs has thus become significantly important, they are more important than any other single subject. Thus, it is natural for aspirants to feel anxious when they are deciding on how to go about them or how to plan studying them. It is also not helpful that they have too many resources to pick from and then the eternal doubt, "How to make notes from the newspaper and how to make notes for current affairs?"

Let us come to first things first, how to plan or strategize studying current affairs and in turn the newspaper. A newspaper is very important and essential when it comes to current affairs and even more in fact. For example, newspapers are a good source for most part of your economics syllabus and key concepts keep repeating themselves in the news items like monetary policy, bank rates, inflation, unemployment etc. It is this reason that the first advice mostly given to UPSC CSE aspirants is to pick up a newspaper and start reading it as soon as possible to develop a habit.

It is almost undeniably important and ndispensable, more so at the beginning of our preparation as it makes you aware bout the bigger and larger things, the nacros of various subjects in a short amount f time and it also exposes you to a variety f viewpoints and perspectives. It also has n advantage that while you are preparing, ou'd most likely be exposed to one or two ubjects at a time while a newspaper will eep giving you some bits and pieces of formation about all the subjects.

Another aspect of newspapers which makes them such a wonderful source of knowledge is that they build on a story, so if you see an event, most likely you'd be able to gain knowledge about various dimensions of the event over a few days and see it from a wide variety of lenses. It is thus important to read one.

Now, how to read a newspaper and what is important in it and what can be ignored? Newspaper reading, when you've just begun might take a lot of time, in a few cases it takes as much as 3-4 hours for beginners but that is not even close to ideal.

In an ideal scenario, one must not be giving more than an hour's time to the newspaper and that too this is the upper limit. More than what must be read, it is easier to talk first about what must not be To start with, crime news is of no use, the exception would of course be if it is a crime which has caught national attention an leads to some reforms either in some law or the criminal justice system etc.

Similarly, for entertainment news, exception would be if it is a news item on how entertainment industry is a cultural ambassador for India abroad etc. So, the point is, almost 95% news items in these 2 categories would not be of any significance to an aspirant and thus it makes no sense to give them time.

Then, politics, while it is important for you to aware about the major events taking place in national and state level politics but it doesn't mean you must read every article on political infighting or inter-party rivalries or the like, what you have to focus on is again very conceptual, for example, a news item about a government being overthrown might come with news on politics of all kind but that is not important to you, what instead is the process by which it was done, was there a 'no-confidence motion', was there 'floor test', how was it done. So, again, your focus must be on learning the basics and how things are done than the actual things happening, your interest is in the components that go inside rather than the actual machine.

Then, sports news is also something which almost all the time would be of little use, unless it is about some huge achievement or some big award.

Similarly, it's natural for you to focus more on national and international news than local or state level, exceptions would obviously be there, but mostly national news and international events are the ones to focus on.

Now, that we have discussed about the things which are not that important, let me also throw some light on the few topics or items which are absolutely necessary for you to read.

First, schemes, it goes without saying that for an exam which is to recruit administrators and future policy makers, it is absolutely necessary to test their knowledge on current and past schemes, their features, weaknesses, strengths, performances etc.

It is very important to read about the background of a scheme as well and the context in which it is released, like a poverty alleviation scheme which deals with wage employment must be understood as to why specifically it is designed the way it is.

Schemes are aplenty and new ones keep coming in, but none of it makes them less important as in a developing country like ours with a federal structure that we have, we would inevitably have schemes run by both the Union and state governments. But, having said that, with few notable exceptions, for UPSC CSE, mostly the schemes run by the Union government are more important, so, you may focus more on them.

Then, some departments are more important than others when it comes to what UPSC would ask in the exam. India is a developing country and a sizeable population is dependent on the state and its interventions for its well-being and its livelihood. Thus, departments like Women and Child Development, Social Justice, Education, Health and Family Welfare become more important than others and thus their schemes become more important, similarly, departments like Environment, Forest and Climate Change, Disaster Management, Science and Technology are important because some very huge challenges we are facing are dealt with by these departments. None of this is to say that others are not important but if at all, these are the ones to prioritize.

Then, policies, a policy differs from a scheme in its scope in a way that most schemes are very specific in nature and always try to achieve very well-defined goals, while a policy is more subjective and is like a guiding light which helps in governance. For example, schemes to manage solid waste may be many but they would all be based on or inspired by policy of the government and where does it keep solid waste management in its priorities and what is the policy to deal with it. A policy is like a set of guidelines, which help design better schemes and thus they are very important. They inform us about the way of functioning of a government and their priorities. They are also important as they are the macro indicators of the way of functioning and seriousness of any government.

Thus, it is very important for UPSC CSE aspirants to have good hold and grasp on them. Some of the major ones can be Environment, Social Sector, Employment,

Education, Health, Food Security, Industry, Intellectual Property etc.

Then, India has a very active and empowered judiciary and has a history of revolutionary judgments. Many of them gave shape to how our democracy functions and thus to keep an eye on the Supreme Court's and High Court's judgments on constitutional matters is important. One has to be mindful enough to know that it is not important to follow all cases in which the government is a party but those where a decision is to be taken on sanctity of a constitutional provision or on a scheme or decision of the government which has any impact or will have any impact on the rights or duties of the citizens or alters or effects the Constitution. Ours is a very vibrant judiciary and an evolving democracy, which makes this institution even more important for the people and what is important for the people, it is important for the administrators or those who want to become one.

Then, there are topics which are almost in their entirety dependent on current affairs and thus the newspaper for their coverage. They are mostly to do with topics which tend to remain in news and are very dynamic. Major things to be covered under such topics are, first and foremost International Relations and International news. Global events are very far reaching at times, in their scope and any answer written must contain the current scenario with respect to the IR in question else it would not fetch good marks.

For example, if you are to make notes of India-US relations, it is important to note down any changes or events happening with respect to the relations between the two nations. Similarly, any note on a global event like a coup in a country or a major decision taken by a multilateral organization will also come from newspapers only. It goes without saying that these are very dynamic topics and must be constantly updated.

Then, another very current affairs-oriented topic is technology, it is almost clear by its name; technology is the latest application of science. While science and technology both are a part of the syllabus of UPSC CSE, the exam has mostly been about technology and rarely would it ask any question on Newton's Laws of Motion. More specifically there are areas in technology which must be kept a regular tab on, these areas are again very dynamic and can go from extreme importance to relative obscurity in a matter of months. It is thus important to give them due consideration. Like Space technology, Nuclear technology, Gene Editing technology etc. are almost evergreen topics and must be followed but certain specific ones like the Nobel Prize awards that year are important.

Lastly, a very current affairs driven topic is environment, though the concepts and static portion has come to be well defined, as it has come to occupy a position of almost a full-fledged subject in its own right, a lot of things keep on happening and new technology, discoveries, findings etc. keep coming, making it a very current oriented topic.

Another major subject, though it has a very big static syllabus to be covered is Economics. As a matter of fact, economics can over the course of preparation of 6-8 months, be revised in its entirety from the newspaper. The reason being, economics' concepts, the ones from macroeconomics at least, keep on repeating themselves again and again in the news. Inflation, unemployment, growth, income etc. are all recurring themes in economics and keep on coming in news. More than this though, economics is a very dynamic topic and the current economic scenario of a country is very important to be understood to write anything on any scheme, policy, intervention etc. of the government.

Making notes is an exercise in interlinking, what it means is that a static syllabus is not supposed to be separate or studied in isolation from the current or dynamic portion of the syllabus. It is to be understood at the very start and there is in fact almost never, a completely and solely static portion, that is to say, a portion without the need or capacity for being updated. Anything, from a strictly historical topic like Indus Valley Civilisation in history to Plate tectonics in Geography become a current one if only they are in news due to some discovery or finding etc. related to them. This would mean that they would need to be updated and the latest discoveries and findings be added to the relevant areas. What must be done while you update these is that you do them at the same place where you made notes of these topics in the first place so that you get all the updated information at one place and in one go. Then there are topics which beg to be updated and will surely not fetch you even average marks if not updated to latest events. Mostly these are topics such as Indian polity, if for example, a SC judgment in a constitutional matter which alters or adds to the understanding of any provision of the Constitution it becomes an extremely important matter in its full context.

Similarly, if the Indian government was to change the way it defines or classifies 'poor people', then, the latest definition of poverty becomes extremely important, much more than the older ones.

It goes without saying that these topics or areas need constant updating and that any older version, if at all, can cost marks than getting you any. The right way of updating the notes of such topics is the same as discussed above, right after the last you wrote about them. Not only does it make them chronologically sound and easy to read but also gives them the right logical flow.

It is a constant part of any topper's advice to interlink the static and dynamic portion of the syllabus, what do they mean when they say so? Simply put, it means to always have a perspective which sees the topic in the light of current situations and development or standing. For example, a topic like Five-Year plan and India's approach towards development might sound like a static topic and a historical one but it must also be studied and understood from the perspective of current economic conditions and scenarios. As in, what could be the possible reasons for India's current economic scenario and how is it to be traced in the FYPs.

Not that you'll have to do this exercise for each and every topic, as it is not even possible to do it for all of them but for certain topics and subjects, which are dynamic and current affairs oriented. It is advisable to have an open mind and think and question things.

Constant updating of notes is something which you'll continue doing but again, this is not an issue like it's made into. You would anyway be reading the newspaper for your current affairs and you would also be following some or the other magazine for current affairs. All you'd be required to do is to ensure that you write whatever you feel is important for any topic in the relevant section in the notes of that topic.

If you haven't yet made notes, just underline the thing in the magazine and update it in the notes when you'll revisit it in the future for revision. For example, if you read something very important on monetary policy in the newspaper and you feel it should be written in the notes then there is no need to write it down separately, just write it down where you've made notes about monetary policy before, this way you'll have everything related to one topic at one place. What this would do is not just save you the hassle of looking up notes or points on the same topics at different places but also help you in updating your notes as you go.

Let's Make Notes and Revise Notes

Now that we have discussed in detail all the components needed to make good notes, I feel it is best that I show you how to go about making notes by actually doing it. We will take up a sample topic from an open source on a topic in the syllabus and will try to make notes from that topic.

Let us start, below is a writeup on a topic taken from Wikipedia:

"Swachh Bharat Mission (SBM), Swachh Bharat Abhiyan, or Clean India Mission is a country-wide campaign initiated by the Government of India in 2014 to eliminate open defecation and improve solid waste management. Phase 1 of the mission lasted till October 2019. Phase 2 will be implemented between 2020–21 and 2024-25.

Initiated by the Government of India, the mission aimed to achieve an 'open-defecation free' (ODF) India by 2 October 2019, the 150th anniversary of the birth of Mahatma Gandhi. The objectives of the first phase of the mission also included eradication of manual scavenging, generating awareness and bringing about a behavioral change regarding sanitation practices, and augmentation of capacity at the local level. The second phase of the mission aims to sustain the open defecation free status and improve the management of solid and liquid waste. The mission is aimed at progressing towards target 6.2 of the Sustainable Development Goals Number 6 established by the United Nations in 2015.

The campaign's official name is in Hindi. In English, it translates to 'Clean India Mission'. The campaign was officially launched on 2 October 2014 at Rajghat, New Delhi by Prime Minister Narendra Modi. It is India's largest cleanliness drive to date with three million government employees and students from all parts of India participating in 4,043 cities, towns, and rural communities. At a rally in Champaran, the Prime minister called the campaign 'Satyagrah se Swachhagrah' in reference to Gandhi's Champaran Satyagraha launched on 10 April 1916.

The mission was split into two: rural and urban. In rural areas 'SBM - Gramin' was financed and monitored through the Ministry of Drinking Water and Sanitation;

whereas 'SBM - urban' was overseen by the Ministry of Housing and Urban Affairs.

As part of the campaign, volunteers, knownas 'Swachhagrahis', or 'Ambassadors of cleanliness', promoted indoor plumbing and community approaches to sanitation (CAS) at the village level. Other activities included national real-time monitoring and updates from non-governmental organisations such as The Ugly Indian, Waste Warriors, and SWaCH Pune (Solid Waste Collection and Handling).

The government provided subsidy for construction of nearly 110 million toilets between 2014 and 2019, although some Indians especially in rural areas choose to not use them. The campaign was criticised for using coercive approaches to force people to use toilets. Some people were stopped from defecating in open and threatened with withdrawal from government benefits."

Now Lets us try and make notes from the above writ-up.

> "Swachh Bharat Abhiyan- ODF Free India by 2019 (Urban- MoH&UA and Grameen- MoDW&S)(phase 1- 2015-19 & phase 2 - 2021-25).
>
> Modelled as a movement, inspired by 'Satyagraha', as 'Swachhagraha'.
>
> Aim: Eradicate manual scavenging, toilet construction, creating awareness about sanitation and behavioural modification."

Now, this is just an example on how to extract important information from a write up or a topic and write it in your notes. In a seemingly very big write-up of around 400 words, there is no more than 40 words worth of important information.

This is how you would like to proceed when you start your notes making exercise. With all the points in the back of your mind, you should be able to make concise and crisp notes, easy to read and easy to revise. With notes ready, it is also important that you keep a very crucial thing in your mind from the very start, this or any exam preparation is not possible if you don't have a strategy that lets you revise your information from the very beginning of your preparation.

UPSC CSE is infamous for its vast syllabus, trust me, many aspirants don't even start their preparation and quit just after looking at the syllabus. It is extensive and covers a very huge portion of all the subjects of everyday inquiry.

It requires an engineer to study history, a doctor to study polity, a historian to have some knowledge of science and much more. It is thus very important that as soon as you study any topic of the syllabus, you have a strategy in place which lets you revise what you study regularly or you'll end up forgetting everything in a matter of few weeks and because the preparation is spread over a few months, it is possible for you to remember nothing more than what you studied in the 2 months leading up to the exam.

At the same time, since it is also impossible to read the books again and again for revision, it is very important to have your notes handy. This is why it is important to have your own crisp notes. When you revise a topic, it would not take you the same amount of time it took when you read it for the first time, it won't even take you the same effort, more so when it is a conceptual topic, but all this has a lot to do with the fact if you are revising directly from the books or not.

I have discussed earlier that a good time table would have revision as an essential component and now that we know how revision is dependent on good notes, it is clear that everything is interlinked. Thus, you cannot take anything lightly, you might think you have a good schedule but then one without time for daily and timely revision would end up being a waste, similarly, you might think you are studying as per schedule and revising but without your own crisp and precise notes, it is not possible.

GS Mains Answer Writing Essentials; The Structure

Now that we have a timetable in place and have also seen how to make notes, revise notes, study from newspaper etc, it is time to move on to the next important component of UPSC CSE preparation.

It would not be an exaggeration to say that GS mains answer writing is the single most important component of this entire exam preparation. GS papers carry 1000 marks and at the same time are common for everyone, even essays give some independence for aspirants to pick from a set of topics but the questions in GS papers are fixed and all of them have to be attempted. It is also the most sought-after component for guidance, most aspirants are confused with almost every facet of answer writing, from 'how to begin' to 'how to write' to 'what to write' etc.

It is almost impossible for an aspirant to do this part on their own and they are fully dependent on coaching institutes or the mercy of some fellow candidates with more 'experience' than themselves. The issue is, just like any other component, it is possible to develop this on our own. We will see how to begin and continue answer writing and self-evaluate for improvement.

But first, let's deal with what constitutes a good answer. An answer for different GS subjects would have different content but an overall outline is almost identical, at times components might differ but then again at times they might not, so, we can have a generic study of GS mains answer writing components and later use them as per the needs and requirements of questions.

When you are writing an answer in general and an answer for UPSC CSE in particular, you must remember that all that you know, thrown at once in what comes to your mind order is not going to get you anywhere. Order is very important and what is also important is the fact that all the components are not just in order but also in their right composition.

"First Blow is Half the Battle..."

It is no joke what they say about first impressions, though you might have experienced otherwise in your life but in an exam, you will seldom get a second chance to make a better impression once you've spoiled your first. As soon as an examiner starts to evaluate your answers, the very first thing they would read would be the introduction you have written to an answer. They would surely want to and would definitely read the whole answer but the confidence they'd have in your answer is built when they read your introduction.

Also, unlike any other part of the answer, you just can't skip writing an introduction. What is also important to note is that an introduction is not just about setting the tone for the rest of the answer but also to make a great impression, and not just that you know the answer but that you know what is the most important part in that answer and what is the focus area, all of this is what a good introduction should be able to do for you. But, even here you must understand that this is not "one size fits all" strategy and an introduction depends fully on the question asked and the demands of the question.

Still, a good introduction is indispensable. Let me explain this with a suitable example, if I was to answer a plain question on the importance given to "Freedom of Speech and Expression in India's constitution and polity". Then my introduction must contain the article which talks about the right to freedom of speech, it must also talk about importance of the right in general. The introduction may look like this; "The right to freedom of speech and expression is one of the foundational values of a democracy and thus it rightly finds itself a place in the Constitution in Article 19 as one of the Fundamental Rights which are accorded the highest protection. Over the years its scope has widened."

Now, I would not claim that this is the best introduction and you can surely write a better one, but it does the following, firstly, it talks about the article in which the right is mentioned, secondly, it talks about the importance of the right in general, third it ends the introduction with a hint on what can be expected in the main body.

This is another key, the question clearly asks about the importance of the right in India's constitution and polity and all of this has to be discussed in the main body and ending, the introduction with the scope of the right information does exactly that. It gives the hint of this being discussed in detail. This creates the right expectations in the mind of the examiner and he knows what to expect.

Once you are done with the right introduction, the next step is the most important part of your answer, the main body. This portion of the answer carries the maximum weight, not just in terms of content or words but also in terms of marks. What you write in this portion matters the most but what also matters is what you don't write and how you write what you do. The main body is where most of the ideas, points etc. are to be written but there must be some ground rules in how you approach this main body. Some of the most important ones are as follows:

1. Your Primary Task is to Write what the Question Demands and Asks and not what you Know

Many times, a well-prepared aspirant would find themselves with more content than they can fit in a 250-word answer.

They would thus try to write everything they know about a topic, which of course is not the right way to do anything. Then, at times they would also write whatever they know about the topic and feel is more important even though the question is talking about maybe a lesser 'important' aspect of the topic.

2. The Most Important Points Must Come First

GS mains is a subjective paper and a lengthy one too, thus, it is possible that an examiner might in turn judge your judgement based on what you feel is more important for a topic and what you feel is of lesser value.

For example, for a question which asks you to write on 'Right to Equality' as enshrined in the Constitution, you might very well write about the Preamble, but if you for any reason focus on your answer on the same, you won't be getting good marks, as the main points must be around fundamental rights.

3. Word Limit and the +– 10% Rule

All the questions have a word limit which tells you to restrict your answer to the same. Now, it is practically impossible for anyone to adhere to it in letter but in spirit one must.

Thus, a safe way to see the same is to check, if you fall in the range of 10% on either side of the given word limit. For example, a word limit of 200 words can see you write 180-220 words and you can expect to be safe from any deductions.

4. Precise and Concise

This point keeps repeating itself but that is only because it is extremely important, and when it comes to the main body of the answer, one can't be expected to afford to beat around the bush.

What instead is required of an aspirant is to come straight to the point. He is expected to bring focus to the main issue in the question wants the focus to be and only in the conclusion, can he focus shift towards a neat summary. Similarly, since word limit is an issue, it is only justified if it is expected that the aspirant would be wise enough to use the prescribed word limit to his/her advantage.

5. Content is King

No matter what your presentation style is, no matter if you are to the dot in following the word limit, no matter what the sequence of the points is, if your content is not up to the mark, there is no chance of getting good marks. Content enrichment is the whole preparation about anyways and we would deal with it, in detail, in the next chapter.

Thus, after a short and crisp introduction and a well-defined body, keeping in mind the points discussed above, one is expected to conclude the answer.

It is true that the first impression is very important but the last one is also no less. It leaves a mark on the examiner as it is the last thing they read and it is fresh on their minds. It is possible that you write an excellent answer but a small mistake with the conclusion costs you. But, before we proceed to the details of a good conclusion, one must understand that ending is not equal to conclusion. You will surely have an ending but not necessarily a conclusion.

A conclusion is arrived at; basically, the whole purpose is to arrive at a conclusion after carefully examining or discussing all the relevant points in the main body.

Thus, a conclusion can't be divorced from the main body; it must flow from the same. A conclusion is thus bringing to a sensible close the topic of concern.

A few important points that must be kept in mind while concluding are:

1. Conclusion must flow from the main body and must be based on careful examination of the points as discussed in the body.
2. The conclusion must be short and should not come to have a whole body of its own, otherwise it will look like a continuation of the points and the main body.
3. The conclusion must not be abrupt or absurd. It should not end in a way that it makes the examiner look for more or wonder if you still have something to say.

4. A good conclusion shall in most cases be optimistic, it shall be based on the examination of all the negative points as well but would try to give a way forward.

Thus, the three essential components have their own distinct importance and all of them demand an equal amount of respect. One must not take any of them for granted.

Content for a Good Answer, Books and Presentation

For writing good content, it is very important to read good content. There are just too many books and study material sources available for each and every topic of the syllabus. It is also very common for aspirants to waste months in just finalizing what all they need to study, which is huge waste of their valuable time. Most aspirants get confused as they try to follow or at least go through sources told by multiple people or coaching institutes. Now, the issue here is that almost 90% of the sources as told by toppers, institutions remain the same, the difference is only with the few value addition sources and even if it is not the case, any of the alternatives are equally good.

For example, for geography, if you are to refer to the books recommended by toppers, you'd find that NCERT textbooks are common and everyone would suggest the same but then a few more reference books would also be in the list. Now if you would look at any other such list, you'd find the same pattern. What you must understand is this, that the NCERT textbooks are the more important component of the booklist for geography and it doesn't really matter which reference book you follow.

Most books are more or less the same when it comes to content on factual topics, and the concepts are so trivial and straight forward that they are in most cases fairly easy to understand and any book can be used to study them. Most topics are only up to general awareness level and NCERT textbooks and 1-2 reference books will more or less suffice. Which standard book to follow, you may blindly pick any one list and start with that, all lists will have some advantages and some gaps, which can be filled at the end of the preparation anyway.

I have over the course of this book, mentioned multiple times, the importance of being to the point, of being concise and precise. I would again say this, there is no need for one to say for the sake of word limit, in case one does not have much content, to beat around the bush. An examiner would if anything, never welcome such an approach. Keep these things in your mind for the content for your answers:

1. Know What is and What is Not Important

It is always important to know what is important, but it is equally important to know what a waste of time and energy is to study unnecessary topics, books etc.

Let me give you one example, there has always been a plethora of magazines which have existed for ages now, all come with interviews of toppers and selected candidates every year and each of it claims to be the best and indispensable for the preparation.

So much so that many aspirants buy multiple issues of these magazines and when they are not able to cope up with the huge pile they have collected, they get discouraged and start slipping up. If one is to do proper research, one can easily see that no specialized study material is needed for preparation.

Only NCERT textbooks, some reference books, one newspaper is enough. But the market is flooded with too much material and when there is too much material, the fear of missing out on something important drives students and aspirants to buy these magazines. Mostly, these magazines are read for interviews of toppers who mostly say how these helped them in their preparation. Maybe they did help them, not commenting on that, the whole point is, they are not needed and can be done away with.

Aspirants need not hoard unnecessary books or magazines, it is waste of precious resources and time. The second part of the same point is that once we decide to prepare, enough time must be given to know what exactly we are going to study and for what topic. We must fix our resources and then give our best to cover them as honestly as possible.

I would say that most aspirants who begin preparation, in the first month at least, are highly motivated and inspired but these small things, wrong guidance, sheepishly following every other guy, trying to do too many things at a time, these things affect them very adversely.

Extending this argument to answer writing. Always know that any particular topic will have more material than the word limit mentioned and that you would be knowing more than the word limit mentioned. In this case, it is obvious to know what is important and what is not. It is extremely important that you write the most important points at the beginning and not 'save' them for the end. It is also important to ensure that your answers are focused on the demands of the questions and not on what you know on the topic.

2. Be to the Point

No one ever likes anyone who beats around the bush and refuses to come to the point. This is the same when it comes to your answers, you must not waste a lot of time, space and content to build up the narrative, you must not spend too much time on introduction and you must not think that with some flowery language, you'd be able to get away with mediocre content.

It is absolutely essential for you to make a very crisp introduction and come to the point of the main body. Also, while you try to explain or elaborate in the main body, don't try to write an essay on everything that you know well, it won't be of any help.

3. GS Like and Not Specialist

Probably one of the more crucial points while we write our answers is to remember that while we are writing GS answers, they must not sound like coming from an expert but from someone with a general level of awareness. This is not to discourage good points but to stress on the fact that GS answers must not sound like optional subject answers, they must not sound editorial like. A general level of awareness is something which is expected from someone who reads the newspaper and is up to date on the happenings and events around them.

4. Breadth and Not Depth Matter for GS Answers

Why is it that it is said and advised to have a different type of answer for GS and Optional papers? The major reason is that level of understanding and the kind of perspectives that are expected of you to be aware of when you are dealing with either papers. While you are dealing with optional papers, it is expected that you would be focusing more on the depth of the issue and that your understanding about the topics would be of someone who knows them in and out, similarly for GS answers, it would be expected that your answers would be more focused on breadth and about multiple dimensions.

5. Small Sentences and Simple Language

Many aspirants, especially those who have not had their education in English medium are most of the times concerned about their writing skills. One of the key issues is that their sentences are too simple and more often than not too short. Well, this is really not a concern to be honest. If at all this is an advantage.

Having the ability to write simple sentences and short sentences is a very rare thing and it can benefit you immensely. It is always desirable that you write in short and small sentences which are easy to understand and comprehend. The short sentences that you will write would make the task of the examiner easier and would also make your answers appear to have come from someone who has a clarity of the concepts.

It would also make for a pleasant read, always remember, language does not define content.

6. Short Paragraphs

I couldn't stress more on the fact that your answers must not look like they are stories. They must be very easy to read, one must not feel lost while reading them, which is highly likely if you are writing huge paragraphs.

The problem with long paragraphs is not just that they are harder to read but also that they are, simply put, an indication of lack of understanding of the concept. If one indeed knows the concept well, it is expected that he or she would be able to explain or put forth his/her points in short sentences or small paragraphs. This is what has come to be known as the 'Feynman Technique' named after the famous theoretical physicist, Richard P. Feynman. Though his technique was about learning any concept, it is equally applicable to putting it across well. What he says is this, that if you know or understand a concept well enough, you must be able to make a child understand it. Writing short paragraphs is a clear sign that you know the details well enough.

7. Use of Key Words

Let me explain this point by giving an example, that I was to say answer a question on the definition of foreign policy, asking what does foreign policy stands for. Now, what you need to understand is this, an examiner is checking many copies, and thus he or she is short on time, thus, what they would do is that they would start looking for keywords in your answer. In the above example, keywords would be 'National Interest', 'set of rules principles', 'relations with other nations/ states', 'influence behaviour', 'promoting and protecting own interests' etc. If the examiner sees one or more of these points, he/she will believe that you are aware of the core concepts. They are also important as they are more often than not a bit technical in nature, which again gives weight to your answers. It is necessary to have these words, to differentiate on how you perceive things and how a layman would do.

If all these points are kept in mind, the content for your GS answers would surely be enough to get you excellent marks.

Value Addition

In the previous chapter, we have seen in detail, the conventional and essential components of good answer writing. All of these points must be kept in mind and with enough practice you'll be able to bring all these dimensions to your answers. But, these points, while very important and essential, they are just not enough to get exceptional marks. Well, at least not anymore. Most selected candidates would tell you that they use certain tools to get more marks and to make their answers more appealing, not just in a visual sense but also in academic sense. It enhances the good points and takes the attention to the points which are most important to the question. These tools also help in managing word limit well, since they can help you explain at times quite lengthy topics in a very concise manner. These tools are also important as they convey that you are able to portray your knowledge in a creative manner and also present information in the way it is supposed to be, for example maps and diagrams. These tools are also important to add value to the content in a way that enhances the presentation, like a suitable example or some data point.

It is thus very important that you develop a habit to incorporate these ideas and value addition techniques in your answers from the very beginning. Some people might find it easier than others to incorporate them but with enough practice, it's absolutely possible for anyone to use these tools.

Let us now see all these tools individually and try to come up with ways and methods to use them more effectively and efficiently.

1. Flow Charts

The first tool that we are going to see is a flow chart. These are very basic charts which are mostly used to describe anything with a chronology or a flow. For any process, a flow chart is a very good way to make things concise and give them a logical flow. If you are to use normal paragraphs for the same amount of content, not only would it take such more space, but, at the same time, it would take a lot of effort on the part of the examiner to connect the points, even when written in a chronological order, a flow chart saves time and effort. For an example, you may see the chapter 3, on making notes.

2. Diagrams and Maps

It goes without saying that a diagram adds value to anything with a visual dimension to it. It is also valid enough and justified enough to expect to see a few diagrams when the context demands one. Like while we were in school and used to study cell structures, an answer without a diagram of the cell structure would not get us any marks. The same principle applies here as well. Not that the importance is the same but yes, nevertheless, it is there and since every single mark counts, it is only right to get this practice going. Similarly, maps are very important when it comes to geography, more so when it comes to economic geography.

For an example you may like to see the chapter on making notes (chapter 3).

3. Data Points, Committees and Commissions

Data points are very crucial, in topics like development, social sector, poverty etc. They add authenticity to the point you are trying to make. Otherwise, it is just a random opinion. Similarly, once you add a name of an expert committee or a commission, formed to give recommendations or studying a particular issue, you add value by proving that your points are in sync with the experts in the field. Not to say that your opinion can't differ, but even so, expert committees and their recommendations help. For example, an answer on the topic of Banking reforms, would get a lot more weight to it if it was supported by points and recommendations by say, the Narsimhan Committee.

4. Names, Examples, Anecdotes

Names and examples are always a good way to put forth more clarity about a point one is trying to make. It is always better to have an example to illustrate your point better. I have in the course of this book, used examples wherever I could, that was done to give more clarity to the point I was trying to make. Similarly, anecdotes, mostly in GS Paper 4, Ethics paper are very important and useful. More so, anecdotes from the real lives of either famous personalities or even your own life are very good for illustration purposes. The personal connect in GS paper 4, which is crucial for testing your personality and ethics, do what all the content would not, they provide authenticity and originality. They also tell that you are willing to learn from your own and other's experience.

It goes without saying that for you to include all of the above in your answers, you'd need a lot of practice.

Random Thoughts

Now that we are approaching the finish line, I would want to talk about certain things which are not directly related to UPSC CSE but, in my opinion, would be of some help.

First, I would like to take up certain doubts, those which are most frequently raised by aspirants and those which make them most restless.

To begin with, this exam is very taxing and the process itself is very exhausting, I mean the exam itself lasts an entire year from prelims to the final result, post personality test, and add to that the fact that an average aspirant would begin preparation a year prior to the prelims. It means that a minimum of 2 years are spent on this exam.

Thus, to maintain enthusiasm and interest is not a small task. Until and unless you are passionate about either the services or the subjects that you are studying, you will find it tough. How is it then possible, to maintain a level of energy which lets you stay ahead?

The simple answer would be to have seek an answer from within. Simply put, why one wishes to do anything is a very personal matter and my motivation or inspiration can't be just borrowed. There can be similar yes, one wants to serve the nation and so does soon else as well but why one wishes civil services to be the medium or why one feels that this service would do justice to his/her abilities or why one finds it the most attractive medium might very well differ.

Now, it is possible that even these may be same but they are what I call as impersonal motivation, in the sense that they come with the very nature of the services. What one needs to find is a very personal or even a very private motivation, it may be something very specific, coming from something one has seen or witnessed. It can also be something what others might call shallow, like making your parents proud and happy and being the reason for their happiness.

Some might say that it is not shallow, and I agree but then many think that motivation to become a civil servant must be service of the nation, I agree again, but not everyone can stay motivated by the big goals, at that times it is those who are around us and their well-being which motivates us. It is indeed tough to 'see' the nation but yes we can easily 'see' our parents and thus their happiness. The point should be to see how this motivation can help you achieve what you want to in order to make you able to do what you want to.

I did have a ritual while I was preparing and I feel that it would help almost everyone. Whenever I used to feel demotivated or lazy or anything like that during my preparation, I would go and just quietly observe my mother while she was working at home. I would see her working as hard as she has always done, ever since I have seen her, waking at 5 and working till late night, from cooking to cleaning to everything else, without any help and without a single complaint. I would ask myself how can you be so selfish, you can't work for a couple of months for the woman who has given her life to make you what you are? Can't you work when in fact she has supported you in every decision of yours, no questions asked and when preparing for this exam was also your decision? It always worked. I would be in my chair in a few minutes, full of energy. This is just my personal example and, like I said, these motivations can't be just copied, you may have your own story and would want to do something your own way.

Then, another very common doubt or query which is asked by aspirants is, how has my life changed after getting into the services? Well, it indeed has changed and of course for the better. The biggest change of course is the sense of responsibility which has come, towards the people. Every action is supposed to be done keeping in mind the greater good of the people. It is also important to note that power does come with the service but responsibilities far outweigh the power. Then, another very important change is the fact that I have this wonderful opportunity to help so many young aspirants who wish to serve the country as civil servants. I enjoy helping aspirants and this has been one of the biggest satisfactions of my post selection life so far.

Another thing which I would like to mention is that being part of the system, the same which we see from outside is a very different experience. It makes you see things from various perspectives, things which one would criticize without thinking twice and may be rightly so, once in the system, you know the actual reason for it being in that shape and you realise, at times, it is just not possible. Thus, you become humbler.

In the end, I would like to say that Civil Services in general and the IAS in particular offer you perhaps the best possible avenue to bring positive change. It is indeed tough but like I always say, nothing worthwhile ever came easy.

If you wish to be a part of the most illustrious of the bureaucracies in the world, one which has served the nation for decades, has given officers who led the formation and reformation of bodies like the Election Commission of India, the Reserve Bank of India, the Central Vigilance Commission, the Central Information Commission, the Union Public Service Commission, the Comptroller and Auditor General of India and many more, you must be ready to make some sacrifices. You must remember that the institution you wish to join is a glorious one as any institution and that its legacy is huge, thus, the amount of hard work it needs you to do is also no less. The reward must justify the pain and, in this case, it does so very well.

Some Fun while Preparing

UPSC CSE preparation can be very exhausting and it is always good to have something which can add some fun to your preparation and what better if the fun is also helping in your preparation.

First, being a book lover, I would list a few books which would give you various and differing perspective about bureaucracy in India and its history. You may like to read one or two of these:

1. "The Steel Frame: A history of the IAS" by Deepak Gupta

2. “Everything you ever needed to know about the Bureaucracy but were too afraid to ask” by T.R. Raghunandan
3. “What ails the IAS and why it fails to deliver” by Naresh Chandra Saxena
4. “Bureaucrazy gets crazier” by M.K. Kaw
5. “The Service of the State” by Bhaskar Ghose
6. “Portraits of Power” by N.K. Singh
7. “Journeys through Babudom and Netaland” by T.S.R. Subramanian
8. “V.P. Menon: The unsung architect of Modern India” by Narayani Basu
9. “Anglo Indian Attitude: The Mind of the Indian Civil Service” by Clive Dewey
10. “The Ruling Caste” by David Gilmour
11. “The Men who ruled India” by Philip Mason

These books are, not at all necessary from the point of view of clearing the exam but then reading only the syllabus and books related to that can be a bit boring. These books are not just informative but also exciting to read as they talk about the service you aspire to join.

In the age of TV/Web Series, it is natural that aspirants would also be watching something or another on some or the other platform.

There are many wonderful series, old and new, which would add a lot to your knowledge and give you insights into wide variety of topics.

I have watched them over the years, some of them while I was preparing, mostly on YouTube, back then, Netflix etc., was still not that big a craze and since I was a student, I had no money to waste on these subscriptions.

Some of the finest series which all aspirants can watch are:

1. Men of Ideas, BBC (YouTube)
2. Harvard Justice series (YouTube)
3. A history of Ideas, BBC (YouTube)
4. In our time, BBC (YouTube)
5. The Great Philosophers, BBC (YouTube)
6. Cosmos: A personal Voyage by Carl Sagan (YouTube)
7. Civilisation: A personal View by Kenneth Clark, BBC (YouTube)
8. The Ascent of Man by Jacob Bronowski, BBC (YouTube)

Though I can't stress enough on the fact that one needs to be very disciplined. At times even one episode every day could also be too much, more so for working professionals. Thus, you should be watching them only after you have met your targets and are on track.

In the end, I would say that give it your best, be honest to yourself and you would surely get through. Wishing everyone all the best, Do well!